the library of african american arts and culture

blues

Its birth and growth

"Mother of the Blues"
Ma Rainey with her
Georgia Jazz band,
Chicago, 1923.

the library of african american arts and culture

blues

Its birth and growth

howard elmer

rosen publishing group, inc./ new york

With gratitude to the known and unknown music makers of eternity who, with African musical influences and roots, have brought us and continue to bring us remarkable music.

Published in 1999 by The Rosen Publishing Group, Inc.
29 East 21st Street, New York, NY 10010

Copyright © 1999 by The Rosen Publishing Group, Inc.

First Edition

Library of Congress Cataloging-in-Publication Data

Elmer, Howard.
    Blues : its birth and growth / Howard Elmer.
        p. cm. — (The library of African American arts and culture)
Discography:
Includes bibliographical references and index.
    Summary : Traces the origins of blues music, its evolution in the United States, and its influence on jazz and rock and roll..
    ISBN 0-8239-1853-X
    1. Blues (Music)—History and criticism—Juvenile literature.   [1. Blues (Music)—History and criticism.] I. Title. II. Series.
ML3521.E45 1999
781.643'09--dc21   98-43705
                                                                    CIP
                                                                    AC MN

Manufactured in the United States of America

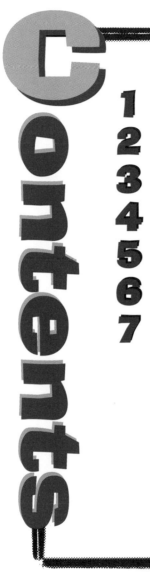

Contents

Introduction

Introduction

Do you have the blues? The kind of blues that makes you feel sad, lonely, down and out? That is one meaning of the term "blues," but not the only one. There is another kind of blues: the musical blues. This kind of blues is by far the better kind of blues to have.

Not too fast, the bass and drums keep a steady beat. The guitar and keyboard mesh just fine—throwing in licks here and there. Listen to that other instrument blowing; is it a harmonica? Wait, there are the horns and a few backup singers. What a groove!

The blues, a type of African American folk music, was born in rural America. It was played and sung before expensive sound systems and recording technology were developed. In the beginning, the blues often took shape in the lonely cry of a single artist and his instrument.

Like its close musical relative, jazz, blues is uniquely American. It is a result of

African music and European music coming together in American society. For example, the "blues feel," an easily recognizable singing style used by vocalists, is a direct result of many African singing styles and song types, including call-and-response, work songs, and field hollers. The subject matter, structure, and sense of the blues came from the experiences of African Americans.

Throughout the years, blues music has been affected by many changes in society. One of those changes was the American Civil War, which lasted from 1861 to 1865. Before the war, pre-blues music had been sung mostly by slaves on Southern plantations. But during the Civil War, the slaves were freed. Freed slaves migrated north, and the music continued to develop in many different areas. In the North, a new style of blues eventually developed: urban blues. This style took root in Chicago and New York. Later urban blues is played by a full band, bringing in the bass, the keyboard, and electric instruments.

Today the blues is often described as the foundation of jazz, soul, and rock 'n' roll. Many performers, both black and white, have utilized the "blues feel" in their music: in the clubs, in the studios, and on the radio. They have taken the blues around the world through tours and recordings and have influenced many other musical styles. Over the years many artists have kept that straight "bluesy" sound, while others have gone on to create new sounds.

The blues has a rich and exciting history. In this book, we will trace the blues from its African origins and see how it grew in America. You will see how blues music has become an important part of African American culture and has influenced music around the world.

well i wish

i was a catfish

Muddy Waters

10

1 before the blues

African music laid the groundwork for the blues. Although African music that came to America can't be traced to just one group of people, the roots of the blues come from peoples of West Africa, including people of the Savannah in northern West Africa.

The Sound of Tradition

Africa has many rich musical traditions. Peoples' instruments, their singing styles, and the important role that music played in their lives all combined to create a unique type of music.

Instruments

The instruments people used depended, in part, on the climate of the region. For example, people in the Savannah (a dry land with little rain) often

The Gbaya use large drums during many ceremonies and celebrations.

used small,
lightweight
instruments (like flutes and stringed
instruments) created from the dry and
sparse vegetation. The instruments
were light because people often
walked long distances while herding
their animals and didn't want to carry
anything heavy.

However, people living in southern West
Africa lived in a different kind of environment.
This area is more moist and has more vegetation
than the Savannah. Because of these conditions,
people were less likely to move around than their
neighbors in the Savannah. They didn't hesitate to
carve out heavy instruments, such as drums, from the
large trees in their environment.

People from both areas of West Africa also used
their own bodies as instruments: clapping their hands
and stomping their feet. This created thrilling and
complex rhythms.

Song Types

Two song types—call-and-response and the

holler—were other important ingredients in African music and in the blues.

Call-and-response, also known as leader-and-chorus, comes from song leaders and choirs in West Africa. During a song, the song leader will call out a phrase in a very loud singing voice. The choir will then respond to the song leader's call with a musical phrase.

Call-and-response can occur between a singer and an instrument, or just between instruments. This style of music resembles the rhythm of conversation: one person speaks, the other answers.

The holler is made up of one musical verse, sung over and over. A holler was often used during work.

Calls, wails, and cries are part of the slow, relaxed style of singing that is common in the holler. The holler can have a long phrase in one breath, a long first note, and then a high-to-low melody along with humming, rasping, growling, wavering, whining, and bending. The holler is also known by many other names: the field holler, the cornfield holler, the field blues, the field cry, or sometimes the street cry.

Music Everywhere

In Africa, music played a very important role in life. Music, dance, and poetry came together in celebrations of birth, initiation rites, marriage, planting and harvesting, and other occasions. Music also was performed on less formal occasions, for recreation and entertainment.

In addition, music was created and spread by African minstrels, known as griots. Griots, who still exist in many African cultures today, sing fantastic stories and praises about ancestry, great events, and people. In this way they are historians and poets as well as entertainers.

A Cruel Change

The histories of Africa and America changed forever when the slave trade began. The slave trade, and slavery, also were important ingredients in the birth of the blues.

The slave trade in the Americas began in August 1619, when a Dutch ship dropped off twenty Africans in Jamestown, Virginia. Over a period of 200 years, approximately 10 to 15 million Africans were taken from Africa and were brought to the New World: North, Central, and South America, as well as the nearby Caribbean islands. About 500,000 of these Africans were taken to what is now known as the

Slaves landing from a Dutch man-of-war at Jamestown, Virginia.

United States of America. The route these slave ships followed is known as the Middle Passage.

Most of the people sold to America were from West Africa. The slave trade was complicated and grueling. The slave ships would travel from port to port until they were jammed full. Then the journey across the Atlantic Ocean would begin. The journey was long and agonizing. It could last anywhere from a few weeks to several months.

During the era of slavery, peoples of the same culture and even family members were separated. Because families, towns, and cultures were disrupted, many parts of African culture, such as religious practices, were lost or changed. In many cases, African cultural traditions were later forbidden in America. People who once had had their own traditions and roles in society were now captives in a society that was unknown to them.

Despite these upheavals and hardships, many of these traditions did survive. And they changed in ways that gave rise to the blues and caused this music to flourish.

2 an oral tradition

How did Africans bring their music to America? Music was not recorded in the same way it is today, neither electronically nor on paper. How then did the music survive? It survived in the minds and lives of people.

In our culture we have become experts at recording information, in the form of letters, books, compact discs, cassettes, films, and videos. However, if these media were not available, what would we have left? People. People are the key ingredient in oral tradition: a spoken tradition passed on from person to person, generation to generation. Music in Africa was, and still is, an oral tradition—it is passed down by word of mouth from mother to child, grandfather to grandchild, teacher to student.

Just as music had played an important role in day-to-day life in Africa, it played an important role in America. Life was hard for African Americans on the plantations and elsewhere. It still was hard after people were freed from slavery. Music, then, was important in helping to establish a rhythm for work, an outlet for pain, and necessary communication with friends.

The Work Song

In daily life, African people sang to the rhythm of the chore at hand. Later, when Africans were brought to America, they modified many of the songs for the many new kinds of manual labor they had to do. These songs were called work or gang songs.

New World work songs were based on the African work songs that came before them. They were the result of slaves on the plantations hearing new styles and themes of music in America and creating something fresh. Even after slavery was abolished, African Americans provided much of the labor needed to maintain the plantations, as well as build the new canals and railroads across the country. They sang their work songs there, too—and in the heat of the day and labor, people shared their musical traditions.

Even when you sing with your family, you're part of a musical tradition that goes back hundreds of years.

Work Song Styles

Work songs usually were of the call-and-response or holler style. They were used when field hands wanted to talk to one another, sing together, or express emotion. By taking turns singing or singing alone, they gave themselves a chance to catch their breath in what could often be grueling hot and humid weather. Singing also gave them an emotional release from backbreaking work.

As people sang work songs, it was common for them to improvise—to make up phrases as they went along. Improvisation leads to variation in the song. You keep the same basic melody or rhythm but change or add to it as you go.

Sometimes these variations are slight. Other times they may make a common tune sound totally different. Variation keeps the song new and fresh.

The work song has clear African roots in its repeated verses, short phrases, and rhythm. Later all of these elements appeared in the blues. The rhythm in the blues, called "swing" or "shuffle," is also known as the "heartbeat" feel (bu-bum, bu-bum, bu-bum, bu-bum). If you listen to the early blues, you can clearly hear some elements of the work song, though with a more danceable rhythm.

Work songs of many styles are still found across the world among people who do hard physical labor.

in the mornin'
well it's early in the mor —
in the mornin'

baby, when i rise,
lordy,
mama

well it's early in the mor —
in the mornin'

a-baby, when i rise,
well-a

The Importance of Oral Tradition

Music was a way for African American slaves and their descendants to communicate with each other on a day-to-day basis. But music also helped people to keep their traditions alive.

This is especially important when you remember that slaves came from different communities in Africa, with different languages and religions. With their music, African Americans were building a new language that was uniquely their own.

3 spirituals

The spiritual is another kind of music that contributed to the blues.

After the early 18th century, when a wave of religious revival called the Great Awakening swept through the thirteen colonies, Christianity became a major force in America. Many African Americans became Christians over the next one hundred and fifty years, learning popular hymns (religious poems based on the Psalms and set to music). To those songs African Americans added their own experiences and singing styles. The result was the spiritual, a kind of African American religious folk song.

The spiritual had a unique purpose for slaves: it allowed them to express their feelings of oppression and hope for a better life. Black Americans identified with the enslavement of the Jewish people as described in the Bible. They used the language describing these events to talk about their own plight. Since it was considered rebellious to speak outrightly of freedom, slaves used words in songs to tell of their thoughts and mistreatment. Words in spirituals such as "freedom land" and "home" carried a double meaning: one directly relating to the song, and the other relating to the slaves' desire to be free or to be back in Africa.

The black spiritual also made use of African singing styles. For example, it often included call-and-response.

Line 1 leader:
They crucified my Lord,
chorus: and He never said
a mumbling word.

Line 2 leader:
They crucified my Lord,
chorus: and He never said a
mumbling word.

Line 3 both:
Not a word,
not a word,
not a word

Worshipper being touched by the spirit during a church service, 1937.

sometimes i feel like a motherless child

a long way from home

a long way from home

Three-Line Stanza

Spirituals had many different patterns of lyrics. One common pattern was the three-line stanza. The three-line stanza later became a hallmark of the blues.

The three-line stanza usually has two similar lines of music or lyrics, followed by a third line that responds and rhymes with the first two lines. However, in early blues the three lines were often the same. The three line stanza would often be improvised while playing. Stock lines (meaning common lines) as well as entire stanzas could be picked up and used in any blues song that felt right.

The three-line stanza sung against twelve bars of music, or the twelve-bar blues, is the most common blues pattern. While other blues patterns do exist, especially in the earlier music, twelve-bar blues is the recognized modern form.

An good example of twelve-bar blues can be found in a famous song, "Cross Road Blues," recorded by Robert Johnson:

Line 1: Standin' at the crossroad, I tried to flag a ride.

Line 2: Standin' at the crossroad, I tried to flag a ride.

Line 3: Didn't nobody seem to know me, everybody pass me by.

Choir singing in a Harlem church.

What is the difference between blues and spirituals? Their structure can be pretty much the same. But while spirituals are concerned with religious faith, "Cross Road Blues" has to do with less religious, more worldly, concerns.

This change of subject did not come overnight—it came during major changes in American society. These changes affected the lives of African Americans, and they also created the right moment for the birth of the blues.

4 the birth of the blues

The blues was born after many different changes happened at the same time. The blues was a new music that reflected new realities in the lives of African Americans.

Freedom

One of these changes was the freeing of the slaves, which came after the Emancipation Proclamation in 1863. The American Civil War ended in 1865.

Some African American music had taken root in the North during the years before freedom arrived, cultivated by free blacks and by

The Emancipation Proclamation.

slaves who had escaped. But when freedom came for slaves, many of them hit the road north, and they took their music with them.

For free slaves in the South, life was somewhat different but also somewhat the same. Even after freedom came, black Americans continued to labor in an unfair sharecropping system. Their music grew into its own style, which you'll read about in later chapters.

New Subjects

As blues music was taking shape, it grew from new subjects that had not been part of spirituals. The music of African Americans was becoming more tuned into worldly concerns. For example, it now celebrated American legends, like that of John Henry, instead of Biblical legends.

Blues is still spiritual—having to do with love, loneliness, and strength—but in the world here on earth rather than the one "up above."

John Henry hammered the mountain

His hammer was striking fire
But he worked so hard,

he broke his poor heart
He laid down his hammer and he died

Where Were the Blues Played?

Blues was spread by wandering singer-performers, or songsters. You can compare them to the griots, the wandering songsters of Africa.

African American minstrels and songsters have had a long history. Minstrels rose out of early colonial times to perform in staged productions and variety shows. These shows began forming around 1800 and continued throughout the century. They had their own music and subject matter, usually taking shape in musical stories such as ballads.

The songsters performed a wide variety of music in different styles. Any place could serve as a stage for a traveling songster: a street corner, a tavern, or a community gathering. Songsters often had instrumentalists to accompany them. But over time, the songsters preferred to accompany themselves. This later, guitar-toting generation of songsters formed a bridge between earlier black music and the blues. By the early twentieth century, as black musicians of the South continued to move north, blues was the music they were playing.

What Are Blues Songs About?

Blues songs are about *everything*.

While a songster's ballad may have been a romantic or adventuresome song about legendary black heroes, the blues usually was about bad times, fears and woes, hard luck, and love (often lost). Blues singers sang of their own hard times. However, they often exaggerated their woes, or gave them a dash of humor. Some blues musicians say that you cannot play the blues properly unless you are feeling blue, and that only by singing the blues can you get rid of them.

Blues singers were some of the first people in America to sing about taboo subjects such as drinking, gambling, jail, and prostitution. (You can see we've now come a long way from spirituals.) And blues became its own form of language, its

Young street musicians; Philadelphia.

own poetry. The whole world was material for the blues—faithless women, reckless men, railroad trains, rambling around, hometown pride, death letters, hot tamales, and even malted milk.

Blues is Recorded

Blues music began to spread faster at the beginning of the 20th century. This happened because blues was starting to be written. Recordings later documented the history of the blues.

One person responsible for the spread of blues music was William Christopher (W.C.) Handy, a minstrel musician. Handy was one of the first people to recognize value in the blues. Handy went on to publish the first blues sheet music, "Memphis Blues," in 1912. When this piece was first played, his band jumped to the top spot among Memphis bands. Handy continued to play an important role in spreading the blues, and in 1926 he published "Blues: An Anthology." He is now known as "Father of the Blues."

At the same time, many African American musicians were still living private lives. One early songster was Huddie Leadbetter, known as "Leadbelly." He was a superb musician who could play hundreds of songs and blues. For much of his life, however, he lived in obscurity.

This changed when Leadbelly was recorded by

W. C. Handy at the piano making notations on sheet music. He wrote the famous "St. Louis Blues."

folklorist John Lomax for the Library of Congress. After he and other blues musicians were recorded, they became famous.

in the pines,
in the pines
where the sun don't ever shine,
i shiver the
whole night
through.

It's hard to say how blues would have survived if people had not started to collect, publish, and record it. Few blues songs were written down, and many might have died along with their performers. Or they would have been passed on through the generations and changed along the way.

Today you can still see the influence these early musicians had on people of later generations. For example, on Nirvana's *MTV Unplugged* album, the last song—the haunting "Where Did You Sleep Last Night"—was originally recorded by Leadbelly.

(left) Leadbelly; (right) Kurt Cobain, lead singer of Nirvana, performing at the MTV Music Awards in Los Angeles, 1992.

5 folk & classic blues

During and after World War I (1914–1917) many African Americans hit the road North, looking for work and trying to leave discrimination behind. African Americans in the North, especially around the larger cities, wanted to hear music from home. Now that blues was being recorded, many record producers saw that they had a market to tap into.

Independent black record labels formed, and black blues artists were encouraged. This helped the growth of folk and classic blues.

Folk Blues

The folk blues, also known as country, down-home, or rural blues, was sung in both southern rural areas and cities. The Mississippi Delta singing style of folk blues is at times almost spoken and is very heavy. Its style resembles that of the work song and the holler. Many similar vocal techniques are used for contrast or emphasis: growling, humming, and using falsetto (a high "false" voice).

Charley Patton was the first Delta musician to give form to the blues. He created the playing style that is now central to folk blues: using the guitar to rhythmically accent the vocal line.

Classic Blues

The first kind of blues to be really popular was the classic blues. Classic blues developed alongside the folk blues of the South and at first was sung mainly by urban women. In fact, women artists were the first to actually bring the blues to broad commercial success through their recordings.

The first blues ever recorded was Mamie Smith singing "Crazy Blues" in 1920. Mamie became famous for her version of this song. Her outstanding singing became the standard that talent scouts across the North and South used to judge other singers.

Many classic blues singers came from the South and had learned the blues there, such as Gertrude "Ma" Rainey, known as the "Mother of the Blues." She was the first blues singer of a truly professional quality. She claimed to have given blues its name after being asked what kind of song she had been singing.

Bessie Smith had been on the road with Ma Rainey, and during her career, became known as "Empress of

A page from Black Swan sheet music, 1923.

the Blues." She is now the most famous of the female blues singers. Her first recordings of "Downhearted Blues" and "Gulf Coast Blues" sold a million copies within the first year!

The classic city blues singers helped establish the blues outside of the South. They also paved the way for the male folk blues artists that started being record-ed in the mid-1920s.

trouble, trouble i've had it all my days.

"EMPRESS OF THE BLUES", BESSIE SMITH

Among them were Lonnie Johnson and Son House. Lonnie Johnson made over 130 recordings, making him the most recorded bluesman of the 1920s. Son House became known for his driving guitar work and emotional vocals. Lonnie Johnson and Son House then influenced Robert Johnson.

Although he died at age twenty-seven, Robert Johnson has become a blues icon. His remarkable sound includes complex guitarwork and aching vocals.

A powerful legend surrounds Johnson—that he had made a pact with the Devil in order to obtain his guitar skill. This probably is a popular story because many of Johnson's songs are about the struggle between good and evil. But whether or not this story is true, Johnson's music has affected every generation of blues players that came after him.

LONNIE JOHNSON WITH BLIND JOHN DAVIS, 1945.

chicago & urban blues

During and after World War II, which ended in 1945, many more African Americans migrated to the northern and western United States. They lived in many of the big cities, such as New York, Detroit, Chicago, San Francisco, and Los Angeles. The popularity of blues continued to grow. Radio stations began broadcasting live or recorded blues programs that anyone could tune into, including a growing white audience.

As the folk blues sound moved to the cities, the urban blues—especially in Chicago—also began to take shape. This robust blues sound reflected the rough times of the Great Depression in many of the larger cities, such as New York and Detroit. By the mid-1930s, a new, harsher sound had emerged: the Chicago blues.

Whereas the classic blues was performed usually by just a pianist and a vocalist, the Chicago

Father of the St. Louis Blues, W. C. Handy, holds his trumpet in his New York music publishing office, 1949.

sound was more complex. A typical ensemble included at least one guitar, a piano, and a stand up bass. This often would be complemented by drums and wind instruments such as the clarinet or trumpet. Some-times the harmonica would replace the wind instruments.

BIG BILL BROONZY, 1937

Adding the Rhythm in Chicago

Big Bill Broonzy, the first king of the Chicago blues, was the first to link the folk and urban traditions. Settling in Chicago in 1920, Broonzy took up the guitar. With Broonzy as its king, the blues continued to grow and make money for record companies in Chicago. During the 1940s, the electric guitar gained popularity and was used by the newest blues players.

One of these new players was "Sonny Boy" Williamson. Arriving in Chicago from the South in the early 1950s, he helped transform the blues sound from rural to urban. He is remembered as an innovator of the harmonica blues. Williamson was among those who recorded with a drummer and created a heavy beat in the music. Strongly influenced by jazz, the addition of a rhythm section led to a musical style that was known as "rhythm and blues," or R&B.

The New Sound: Blues-rock

Muddy Waters, originally from Mississippi, arrived on the Chicago scene in 1943 and influenced the blues-rock sound. He recorded with other bluesmen from the Delta region. He became well known for his talents with the electric guitar—his use of the slide technique in particular.

SONNY BOY
WILLIAMSON

Howlin' Wolf and B. B. King are two other important bluesmen from the post-World War II era. Howlin' Wolf moved to Chicago in 1953, where he was a rival of Muddy Waters. Some say that this competition led blues to new artistic levels. Wolf was known for his astonishing shows. With his six-foot frame, hollering and shouting, romping about the stage, even writhing on the floor, he made quite an impression!

B. B. King is now hailed by rock fans as an original master of the electric guitar. He brought the blues guitar solo to the polished concert venue, and often made both the rock and soul charts with his hits. Today he is known as the "King of the Blues," a superstar popular with both black and white audiences.

Albert King was the first major blues artist to cross the bridge into soul music. He was also the first to bring

HOWLIN' WOLF

43

blues and classical musicians together when, in 1969, he played with the St. Louis Symphony. He was also known for play-ing a right-handed guitar left-handed!

the thrill is gone,
baby
the thrill is gone a

44

These and many other bluesmen became popular during the 1940s and 1950s. Together they are largely responsible for bringing the blues from an acoustic to an electric, or amplified, sound. As they toured and recorded, they served as the link that brought blues into popularity throughout the United States, particularly the white middle class, in the 1960s.

come on over...
i'll play the blues for you

way from me.

ay from me.

ALBERT
KING

new generations of blues

Before the 1950s, the blues had been considered primarily a black folk art. However, in the late 1950s young Americans took an interest in various kinds of folk music, and the blues became popular again. Soon blues had a major impact on early rock 'n' roll and the music that came after it.

The British Invasion

Back in the 1950s Big Bill Broonzy and Muddy Waters brought their style of playing to England, gaining legions of fans. Along with the European-touring American Folk Blues Festival, starring Memphis Slim and Willie Dixon in the 1960s, they influenced a storm of British bands.

These bands came to America in what is known as the British Invasion of 1964. The Beatles, the Moody Blues, the Rolling Stones, the Who, the

The hip hop generation is one of the many descendants of the blues.

Yardbirds and many other bands took over the American airwaves. Some bands, such as The Rolling Stones, played their early songs sounding much like the bluesmen who inspired them. Other bands changed things around. For example, one popular Beatles song, "Twist and Shout," is bluesy in its song structure. But it also has a danceable groove, reflecting the early rock 'n' roll sound of artists such as American smash Chuck Berry.

American Noise

By the time the British Invasion arrived, the American scene had been under the spell of rock 'n' roll for many years. As a result of the popularity of rhythm 'n blues and doo-wop vocal music (and later, the Motown sound), rock was coming into its own—and carrying blues along with it. Elvis Presley already had popularized rock 'n' roll versions of many blues songs, including Big Mama Thornton's "Hound Dog" (a twelve-bar blues). Bob Dylan was popularizing poetic, blues-influenced songs such as those on *Highway 61 Revisited*. People wanted to hear more.

The phenomenon of the British Invasion marked the beginning of a full-scale 1960s blues revival. As British bands climbed the charts, the American scene

Fathers of the British Invasion, from left to right: Little Bill Gaither, Memphis Slim, and Big Bill Broonzy.

49

answered back with its own rash of blues-rock bands and performers: the Allman Brothers, Canned Heat, Captain Beefheart, Credence Clearwater Revival, the Grateful Dead, Jefferson Airplane, and Santana, among others. Each of these bands brought its own background to the blues style: Latin rhythm, white Southern roots, or the new psychedelic sound coming out of San Francisco.

Two of the most famous blues-influenced artists of this period were Janis Joplin and Jimi Hendrix.

JANIS JOPLIN

Acknowledging Bessie Smith as an influence, Janis Joplin was the best known of the white female blues artists. Her live-wire vocals completely transformed any song she was singing—from twelve-bar blues like "Turtle Blues" to jazz ballads like "Summertime" to more contemporary, Country-and-Western songs like "Me and Bobby McGee."

JIMI HENDRIX

Jimi Hendrix is an artist who blurred the boundary between blues and rock. Remembered as the most revolutionary rock guitarist, Hendrix kept himself steeped in the blues. As a result, a song like "Voodoo Chile Blues" (from :Blues) sounds like a blues song, but at the same time it creates a whole new sound belonging to Hendrix alone.

After the blues-rock explosion of the 1960s, the

51

blues continued to be played in America, Europe, and even Japan. Many of the white blues performers of the sixties moved on to revolutionize rock, as the Beatles did with *Sergeant Pepper's Lonely Hearts Club Band*. At the same time, other rock bands with blues influences, such as Led Zeppelin, began to make their mark.

New Directions

With this new outpouring of blues-influenced artists who became rock stars, you may be curious: What happened to the blues scene? Well, it has been growing in many different directions.

Two of the major blues artists who came to prominence after the British Invasion were Albert

Taj Mahal performing at the 25th anniversary of the New Orleans Jazz Festival, 1994.

Collins and Taj Mahal. Toward the end of the 1970s, Albert Collins released a series of blues records that elevated him to near-superstar status. His "icy" guitar sound made him a distinctive voice in the blues revival of the 1980s. Taj Mahal, who recorded a few blues albums in the late 1960s, later combined the blues with both Caribbean and African musical forms. He began touring the world with his new, unique musical style. In Africa he played with many musicians, linking the blues back to its musical origins.

Two bluesmen came to prominence in the 1980s: Stevie Ray Vaughan and Robert Cray. Despite his early death at age thirty-five, Vaughan was an electric guitar innovator whose work pays respect to both Jimi Hendrix and Albert King. Robert Cray also has received much recognition for his blues work, which has strong gospel and soul influences.

One of the hottest blues players right now is Keb' Mo'. Taking home the 1996 Grammy for Best Contemporary Blues Album (*Just Like You*), he followed up in 1998 with *Slow Down*. His music combines the blues tradition with a lyrical folk-pop feel.

Descendants of the Blues

In recent decades, much more new blues-influenced music has been born. But blues also is taking on new sounds. Sometimes these sounds are so different that, even if the early blues players were alive today, they probably would not recognize them as blues! The themes, emotions, and grooves of the blues can be found from pop to funk to soul to heavy metal. Rap also holds a special place as a child of the blues. Like blues, rap is a way for people to express emotions and opinions through music. Both blues and rap came from the experiences of African Americans, and have changed music forever.

Here to Stay

During the past forty years, blues has gained fans from all countries and cultures. Originating in the black American community, the blues appeals to all

Etta James's blues singing spans many decades and styles. She even recorded an album dedicated to the music of jazz vocalist Billie Holiday. Etta's latest album is titled *Life, Love & the Blues*.

ETTA JAMES

classes and races. The blues is an honored tradition, and it still excites new listeners and artists.

As we come close to the one hundreth anniversary of blues, it's clear that the blues—a remarkable music—will continue well into the next century.

i just found me
a bottle of
blues...

Sometimes playing acoustic blues ("I Get Lonesome"), other times taking on a kind of blues-rapping ("Hotwax"), Beck mixes it up by bringing in samples from just about everywhere.

Glossary

blues An African American folk music concerned with loss, loneliness, and taboo subjects.

call-and-response A style of singing in which one person sings and another responds.

Chicago blues (urban blues) A style of blues, originating in Chicago, using heavy rhythm and electric instruments.

classic blues An early type of blues, popularized by urban women vocalists.

field holler (holler) A type of song, often used during work, that sounds like a growl or cry.

folk blues A type of blues, usually sung by a single person, that strongly resembles the work song and field holler.

griot An African minstrel who sings stories about historical and contemporary events and people.

minstrel A kind of traveling performer, popular in the early 1800s, who took part in variety shows.

improvise To make up as you go along.

oral tradition Passing of information and customs by word of mouth.

rhythm and blues (R&B) An offshoot of urban blues which utilizes a heavy emphasis on uptempo rhythm.

rock 'n' roll A type of popular music, originating in

the 1950s, that was influenced by blues.

slavery A social system in which an employer literally owns the labor force.

songster A musician who played popular songs and ballads.

spiritual An African American religious folk music similar in structure to the blues.

twelve-bar blues A form of blues played within twelve bars of music; its verses consist of three-line stanzas.

work song A type of song sung during labor, often requiring improvised verses; often in call-and-response style or of the field holler type.

Discography

Broonzy, Big Bill. *Big Bill's Blues*. Portrait RK 44089

Four Women Blues: The Victor / Bluebird Recordings of Memphis Minnie, Mississippi Matilda, Kansas City Kitty and Miss Rosie Mae Moore. RCA / Bluebird 07863 66719-2

Hendrix, Jimi. *:Blues*. MCA-Chess MCAD-11060

House, Son. *Delta Blues (The Original Library of Congress Sessions from Field Recordings, 1941-42)*. Biograph BCD 118

James, Etta. *Her Best*. Chess CHD-9367

Jefferson, Blind Lemon. *King of the Country Blues*. Yazoo 1069

Johnson, Robert. *Robert Johnson: The Complete Recordings*. Columbia / Legacy C2K 64916

King, B. B. *Singin' the Blues / The Blues*. Flair / Virgin V2-86296

Prison Songs: Historical Recordings from Parchman Farm 1947–48. The Alan Lomax Collection. Rounder Records LC 3719

Rainey, Ma. *Ma Rainey's Black Bottom*. Yazoo 1071

Rhythms of Life, Songs of Wisdom: Akan Music from Ghana, West Africa. Smithsonian Folkways 40463

Smith, Bessie. *Bessie Smith: The Collection*. Columbia CK 44441

Thornton, Big Mama. *The Original Hound Dog*. Ace CDCHD 940

Vaughan, Stevie Ray and Double Trouble. *Texas Flood*. Epic EK 38734

Waters, Muddy. *The Best of Muddy Waters*. MCA-Chess CHD-31268

Williamson, Sonny Boy. *Sonny Boy Williamson, The Bluebird Recordings* (1937–38). RCA / Bluebird 07863 66723-2

Wolf, Howlin'. *Howlin' Wolf / Moanin' in the Moonlight*. MCA-Chess CHD-5908

Yoruban Drums from Benin, West Africa. Smithsonian Folkways 40440

Charters, Samuel. *The Roots of the Blues*. Salem,
NH: Marion Boyars, 1981.

Cohn, Lawrence. *Nothing But the Blues: the
Music and the Musicians*. New York: Abbeville,
1993.

Lomax, Alan. *The Land Where the Blues Began*.
New York: Pantheon Books, 1993.

Oliver, Paul, Max Harrison, and William Bolcom.
The New Grove Gospel, Blues and Jazz. New
York: W.W. Norton, 1986.

Palmer, Robert. *Deep Blues*. New York: Penguin,
1981.

Santelli, Robert. *The Best of the Blues: The 101
Essential Albums*. New York: Penguin, 1997.

Santelli, Robert. *The Big Book of Blues: A
Biographical Encyclopedia*. New York: Penguin,
1993.

Savage, Steve. *The Billboard Book of Rhythm*.
New York: Billboard, 1989.

Sonnier, Austin, Jr. *A Guide to the Blues: History,
Who's Who, Research Sources*. Westport, CT:
Greenwood, 1994.

Southern, Eileen. *Biographical Dictionary of Afro-American and African Musicians*. Westport, CT: Greenwood, 1982.

Southern, Eileen. *Music of Black Americans: A History*. 3rd ed. New York: W.W. Norton, 1997.

Index

a

abolition, 17
Allman Brothers, 50
American Folk Blues Festival, 47

b

Beatles, the, 47, 52
Berry, Chuck, 49
blues-rock, 41, 49
British Invasion, 47–49
Broonzy, Big Bill, 40, 47

c

call-and-response, 12, 18, 21
Canned Heat, 50
Captain Beefheart, 50
Caribbean, 14, 53
Chicago, 39, 42
Chicago blues, 39–46
classic blues, 34–37
Collins, Albert, 52–53
Country and Western, 51
Cray, Robert, 53
Credence Clearwater Revival, 50

d

Dixon, Willie, 47
dance, 13
Dylan, Bob, 49

f

folk blues, 34, 39

g

Great Depression, 39
griot, 14, 27

h

Handy, Willam Christopher (W.C.), 30
Hendrix, Jimi, 50, 51, 53
Henry, John, 26
holler, 12, 18, 34, 42
House, Son, 36–37

i

improvisation, 18, 23
instruments, 11–12
   electric guitar, 40, 43

j

jazz, 41
Jefferson Airplane, the, 50
Johnson, Lonnie, 36–37
Johnson, Robert, 23, 37
Joplin, Janis, 50

k

King, Albert, 43, 53
King, B.B., 42

l

Leadbelly, (Huddie Leadbetter), 30, 33
Led Zeppelin, 52

Acknowledgments

The author wishes to extend thanks to his wife, Christy Ann, for her love; to the guitar-bearing Dan Harsh for showing him how to play the blues; to Odinga Oginga Guy Warren Jr., and Juma Santos, who have drummed African and related musical traditions to him; and to George "Boz" Boziwick, a fantastic blues harp player and composer, for his useful suggestions.

The editors wish to extend a special thanks to music historian Stephen C. LaVere, whose expertise was critical to the successful completion of this project.

About the Author

Howard Elmer is a composer and musician currently residing in New York City.

Credits

Design and Layout

Laura Murawski

Consulting Editors

Erin M. Hovanec and Erica Smith